Petals of Prayers

Written by
Terialina

Illustrated by
Shiela Alejandro

Order this book online at www.trafford.com
or email orders@trafford.com

Most Trafford titles are also available at major online book retailers.

Print information available on the last page.

ISBN: 978-1-4907-9345-0(sc)

978-1-4907-9346-7(e)

Our mission is to efficiently provide the world's finest, most comprehensive book publishing service, enabling every author to experience success. To find out how to publish your book, your way, and have it available worldwide, visit us online at www.trafford.com

Trafford rev. 01/25/2019

www.trafford.com

North America & international
toll-free: 1 888 232 4444 (USA & Canada)
fax: 812 355 4082

For you ...

...this book was made for all of the littles ... all of the littles with lots
of questions, big hopes and lots of love. My prayer for you is that you
learn to pray and pray one prayer every day after reading this book.
this book is dedicated to my son who we call Deuce - may
you always remember to pray daily and never stop talking to
God --no matter how old you get. I love you!
Thank you Jesus for the inspiration to write this
book - to you I give all of the Glory.

"Come on Mommy, this way," Lylah said as she pulled her Mommy's hand in the park.

Lylah and her Mommy stopped for a moment to look at the flowers. "Don't they smell so pretty Mommy?" Lylah asked.

Lylah's Mommy picked a flower and showed it to Lylah.

Holding the flower, Lylah's Mommy pulled off one of the petals.

As she held the petal in her hand she said, "let's say a little prayer Lylah," and then she began to pray, "God, please bless all of our friends and all of our family and keep all of them safe, Amen."

Lylah watched her Mommy very closely as she closed her eyes and prayed.

"My turn!" ...Lylah shouted. Holding the flower, Lylah pulled off the next petal, closed her eyes and began to pray, "God, please bless my Mommy and my Daddy and Leah too, Amen."

Lylah's mommy smiled and began to clap, "Great job Lylah!" Lylah smiled back at her mommy.

"Your turn Daddy," Lylah said as she held the flower with two missing petals up to her daddy.

Lylah's daddy pulled another petal off of the flower, closed his eyes and started to pray, "God, I pray for Lylah to always find happiness in her day and love in her heart and I pray that she always remembers to pray every day, Amen."

Lylah's Mommy smiled at Lylah's Daddy as he finished saying his prayer. Lylah looked down at the flower with only a few petals left and decided to save those petals and prayers for later.

Lylah grabbed her Mommy and Daddy's hands and began to spin around. They all twirled around and laughed together.

On the way home, Lylah and her Mommy and Daddy sang some sing along songs in the car together.

Nighttime came too fast, after reading Lylah's favorite bedtime story, it was now time for her to go to bed.

Lylah asked her Mommy and Daddy if she could say a prayer. They happily agreed.

"God, thank you for giving me the best parents ever and thank you for giving me the best dog ever, I pray that we all live forever and have the best dreams tonight and I pray that you have a good day too God, Amen."

"Amen," Lylah's parents said after Lylah finished her prayer.

"Goodnight Lylah, sweet dreams, we love you," her Mommy said as she tucked her in and kissed her goodnight.

"Goodnight Mommy, Goodnight Daddy, I love you," Lylah said as she slowly drifted off to sleep.

~ SING ALONG SONG ~

~ PRAY WITH ME ~
Would you...
Say a little prayer for me?
And I'll ...say a little prayer for you!
When we pray... we make God Happy.
So, let's say another prayer or two

~ SING ALONG SONG ~

~THANKFUL~

Just ...
Take a little moment to thank him
Thank him for all that he's done for us
Take a little moment to thank him
Thank him for our friends... and our family
Take a little moment to thank him
Thank him for our eyes and the air we breathe
Take a little moment to thank him
Just ...
Take a little moment to thank him.
Thank you, Jesus!

~GOODNIGHT PRAYER~

Dear God,
I come to you tonight to say
Thank you for all that you do for me
Thank you for my family
Thank you for my friends
Thank you for my food
Thank you for my clothes
Thank you for my toys
Thank you for my home
Thank you for always loving me
Please help me to always do good
and to always love and help others
Please forgive me for not always listening when I should
I love you, in Jesus name, Amen.

I am thankful for:

1.

2.

3.

I want to Pray for:

1.

2.

3.

Things that makes me happy:

1.

2.

3.

If you would like to connect with Terialina,
you can find her through the following:

Facebook:

https://www.facebook.com/booksbyterialina/

https://www.facebook.com/terialinaphotography/

Instagram:

www.instagram.com/

terialina ___photography

Amazon:

- Enchanting Starlight

- Petals of Prayers

Printed in the United States
By Bookmasters